ADVANCE PRAISE FOR OF DAISIES AND DEAD VIOLINS

"Sue's laconic, almost impressionistic creative style reminds us of a master short story author from the early 20th century - Japanese writer Akutagawa Ryūnokuke. They both share the passion for describing sights and sounds, that are so depictive they become "three-dimensional". Sue aspires to represent the whole richness of the human emotional palette and the expressiveness of her language results in her graphically creating bright visual images…"

—Oleksandra Osadcha

"Using evocative lines with beautiful images of the season - punctuated with good alliteration giving a staccato bite where needed - S.B. Borgersen's prize winning sonnet will delight any reader."

—**Meg Marsden**, *Writing Magazine*, October 2017

Of Daisies and Dead Violins

Of Daisies and Dead Violins

collected poems by

*

S.B. Borgersen

OF DAISIES AND DEAD VIOLINS
Copyright © 2021 S.B. Borgersen
Cover Image Copyright © 2021 Robert Howie Smith
All Rights Reserved.
Published by Unsolicited Press.
Printed in the United States of America.
First Edition.

No part of this book may be used or reproduced in any manner whatsoever without written permission except in the case of brief quotations embodied in critical articles or reviews. People, places, and notions in these stories are from the author's imagination; any resemblance is purely coincidental.

Attention schools and businesses: for discounted copies on large orders, please contact the publisher directly.

For information contact:
Unsolicited Press
Portland, Oregon
www.unsolicitedpress.com
orders@unsolicitedpress.com
619-354-8005

Cover Design: Kathryn Gerhardt
Cover Image: Robert Howie Smith
Editor: S.R. Stewart

ISBN: 978-1-950730-86-5

Author's note

These poems were written over twenty years. All at times when I just needed to write poetry and nothing else. Some all in a rush, and others gently paced over months.

July 2020

Contents

Allow yourself to drift	16
Always seeking	17
A Man after Midnight	18
A poem about a poem	19
A Sliver of a Nova Scotia Summer	20
A Thought	22
At odds	23
A Valentine from a Scrabble Lover to His Partner	24
A Villanelle to an Unborn Child of Rural Life	25
Blueberry Hill	26
Books at Boarding School	27
Breakfast on Symi	28
Broken Story	29
Buried in the Smoke	30
Catching thoughts and losing baggage	31
Cathedral Grove	32
Closing Time	33
Cracks and All	34
da Vinci's Burlington House Cartoon	36
Death Wish	38
Declaration	39
Dissection	40
dolmades (i)	41

dolmades (ii)	42
Each	43
Emerging Reason	44
Event?	45
Fly	46
Fresh Blood	47
Getting Older	48
Glimpsing a Nova Scotia Autumn	50
He's Still in the Phone Book	51
Hindsight	53
How You Think You Might Find Happiness	55
I am	57
If only	59
Into the light	60
It's Worth Mentioning	61
Journey to a World Away	63
Killer	64
Lament for Nelly	65
Lament for the Future	66
Last Song for George	67
Life	68
Light Bulb Moment	69
Line Up	70
Making up the Numbers	71
Man in a bar	72
Marriage Vows	73

Mauritius Roadside Chili Cakes	74
Mother Nature Speaks	75
Moving On	76
Music of Life	77
My Grandmother	78
Not Fade Away	79
Ode to a Nova Scotia Spring	80
on a beach walk August 2011	81
Once	82
One more time	83
Only O?	84
Pairings	85
Patterns	86
papuros	87
Point of View	88
Postcard from The Western Isles	90
Postcard (for Ma) from Cape Breton	91
Postcard from Prince Edward Island	92
Rameau's Menuet en Rondeau	93
Reading a Poem Before Breakfast	94
Reflection	96
Rejection	97
Resilience	98
River (i)	99
River (ii)	100
River (iii)	101

Sandscript	102
Seize the Day	103
Signals	104
Sister of No Mercy	105
She	106
Solas	107
Something Special	109
Taking the Zig-Zag Ferry in Nineteen Seventy Something	110
Tea Party Madness	111
Tell your children to	112
That's couples for you	113
The Cookery Book Given to You by Your Mother	115
The day my grandfather drowned the kittens	116
The fall at the waterfalls	117
The Feel of Dark	118
The Ghost Writer	120
The last eclipse	121
The Loss of Rosalind	122
The Midnight Bus	123
The Push	124
The Ravine	125
The reading of the will	126
The Ridgeway - the Oldest Road	128
The Song in Your Head	129
The Thinker	130
Third Space Inhabitant (A Sense of Place and Home)	131

Thoughts from the top of the stairs	132
Tick Tock	133
Travel this shore with me	137
Tuesday Morning	138
Twenty-four Hours of Canadian Winter	139
Unbalanced Equation	140
Vanishing Point	141
Verse 4 from 30 verses in 30 days	142
Visiting North Uist: land of my ancestors	143
Wasted on the Young	145
Watching Over You	146
Were You Once an Art Teacher? Really?	147
What would one need in a poem?	149
Who cares but you?	150
Your forest	152
The April 2020 Collection	153
Online/pickup grocery shopping	155
Powerless night	157
Balancing	158
Corona	159
Birthday party	160
Gifts	161
Encyclopaedia	162
Last night	163
Relationships	164
Jumbled	165

This is the time	166
Breviloquent	167
The gift of time for Wendell	168
Baking bread	169
In the grand scheme of things (2)	170
When	171
In that moment — the unfinished poem	172
An April Week in a Nova Scotia Garden	173
St. George's Day	175
The response to the bridge challenge	176
Letters of Distraction	177
Electricity	177
Individual	177
The lesson	178
The Last of the Month	179
Vapour trail	181
Acknowledgements	182
About the Author	184
About the Press	186

For my grandfather
Herbert Arthur Cope
1892 - 1972

who, in his weekly gardening columns,
went by the name
Uncle Remus

✢

and for Jack

✢

Allow yourself to drift

Stories told unfold from
shifting clouds
hinting at transitional action
until

The damselfly with translucent wings
hues of indigo and jade like oil
on water over which she hovers

Skips her mismatched dance
away into the gold of evening

Always seeking

I could never find the words
to tell the truth
or even lie about the restless tide
that rides my mind

I could never take the step
however small
to beat the sliding doors
before they close

Trapped before and yet behind
the dust that veils the eyes
of mankind's blinkered view
however written

In the sun I still am blinded
and disguised behind the shades
that hide the depth of truth
is only mine

A Man after Midnight

She wants to write a song tonight
of men, or money, or mothers,
or kisses of fire
that's the name of the game

The winner takes it all tonight
is it Fernando, or Waterloo
what a super trooper
to take a chance on me

She writes I have a dream tonight
but does your mother know
about Chiquita
and the man in the middle

So now it's voulez-vous tonight
as the midnight special says
thanks for the music
but gimme gimme gimme

a man after midnight.

A poem about a poem

The piano plays a song
without words
I still hear
stories told through octaves and notes
within the highs and lows of sounds
trills and runs, tinkles?
Of laughter?
A joke.
Or not.

A poem can flow over and along
with words
without the song?
I still hear it you know:
the music of lines
with lilts and phrases
pauses and stresses
shapes on pages
perfect choices of this word or that.
Lyrics singing along.
No joke
but I smile all the same

A Sliver of a Nova Scotia Summer

It dawns on you one morning late in June
as mayflowers start their fade:
soon the lady's slipper orchids
will arrive to tell their message
in gentle pink-tinted voices
as if in secret

'summer's on its way'

you know you've yet to see the yarrow
the partridge berry and rhodora
but on the shaded forest floor
painted trillium and Angelica
unfurling ferns and wild iris
let you know for sure

'summer has arrived'

Monarch butterflies arrive in clouds
with ruby-throated hummingbirds
all this way north from Mexico.
Dragonflies and damselflies
flirt hints of purple greens
around still pools

'yes, summer's really here'

wild strawberries and blueberries

for summer picnics on the shore
you feel the soft white sand
beneath your feet and dip
toes in the welcome
clear warm ocean.

and now you taste,
smell, feel, gaze,
hear those gentle lapping waves

of summer

A Thought

It came from the half-price sale
damp and smelling
the thought
a single thought
that age difference does not matter

It doesn't help to reach without thinking
grab that thought again
let the words lick
lickety click

Make no resolutions that will not help one jot
to spot the plot of getting your act together
resolve to hunt out that thought again
and again. It's still there
you know.

At odds

One pink, one orange, one white
I pop them
then drop them
from sight
out of my circle of thinking
ridding my head for this night

Hoping at dawn I will write
of distant existence
for sixpence
I might
find others to match them
in pairs. Of pink, or orange
or white

A Valentine from a Scrabble Lover to His Partner

The empty Scrabble board's before us like a lake
waiting for us to paddle or to drift
with unknown words for me to give and you to take
wrapped in fine tissue, tied in gold, a gift.
To find another single living soul upon this earth
who feels the same, who sees the same
and wishes for a future built together
is like the moment when the lightning brings the truth
for now's the time to forget about the game
and ask you this: will you be mine forever?

A Villanelle to an Unborn Child of Rural Life

You've not yet heard the wondrous songs of birds
nor tasted strawberries in the month of June
the life to come is yours you have my word

Ocean's waves on shores are life's rewards
or lakes to hear the haunting cry of loons
wait 'til you hear these wondrous songs of birds

That's the second now I'll tell the third
of parties where you'll catch bright red balloons
the life to come is yours you have my word

In time you'll find that memories will be blurred
but sharpened with the frosting of the moon
you'll always know the wondrous songs of birds

to fly as you will wish quite undeterred
and sip good wines with friends in afternoons
the life to come is yours you have my word

I'll give you life not idle strings of words
nor feed you sweetness on a silver spoon
You've not heard all the wondrous songs of birds
the life to come is yours you have my word

Blueberry Hill

I should be there
swaying to the tunes and humming
love's sweet haunting memories
but I am waterlogged
bogged
down
with

Thoughts of hills
out of reach
tonight
I search
for missing
lost
unspoken words

A cup of tea? A peppermint?
Will they cure or kill?
Moons don't stand still
or linger in those dreams of truth
and youthful vows

Our far off thrills
are played once more by wind
in willow trees
until they sing
and strum tonight
of Blueberry Hill

Books at Boarding School

They had us read To Kill a Mockingbird by day
and yet by night beneath the bedspreads
in the sharp defining yellow beams
of flashlights
we read Lady Chatterley

Understanding simple truths for those who
borrowed and followed in the reading circle
playing games with forbidden words
flushing with the thrill
or so we thought

Which do we remember most?
Required reading or the secret turning
of leaves at midnight, falling asleep
dreaming of worldly adult acts
between those orange covers

Breakfast on Symi

The sublime hint of pine
in honey drizzled on
bowls of thick yoghurt
with almonds and saporous
toppings

On the tip of the spoon
feel the island's bounties
between lips
on tongue
waiting, savouring long
before the first swallow

Sitting back
breathing the blushing air
apricot gold as the morning rooftops
before the next taste
watching the fishermen in the harbour
squid slapping ink-purple on the dockside
for later prandial orectic feasts

Breakfast is not over
flakes of fresh hot feather-light croissants
oozing with melting bitter-sweet chocolate
sucking fingers not to lose a morsel
before sharpening all senses with
anticipated dark pungent coffee

Broken Story

The skip in the silence
empty rooms of reflection
the slow in the quickstep
the stop
when the lullaby
finally lulls
into slumber

A ghost of the girl who once
played Knights in White Satin
Moody and blue
dancing slowly 'til dawn

These are the pieces
I can't put together

Buried in the Smoke

like my grandfather's briarwood pipe
tracing blue smoke wisps
coils and drifts in spirals
I cling to the balm
of memory in their wake

the penny will keep rolling
travelling out of sight
beyond the point of turning back
with no time to regret the past
or fill our hearts with future

are those tears dry? Is that voice hoarse?
Say goodbye with songs not words
you will be heard by those who want
to dance away the walls

leaving behind more than the smoke

Catching thoughts and losing baggage

Circles in the sky
like brims without hats
skimming thoughts and
words on a page of deep nothing

Forgetting the muddy path beneath
a heath of withered intention
buried deep within
the wilderness of everything

It is time to move on
throw the scarf of abandon
around the necks of those
who mean something

Cathedral Grove

The arboretum calls my name
this day when there is no one
I tread so softly through the trees
with tin botanic latin labels
and glossy leaves fine fronded palms
until I arrive at you.

Are you a tree or another being?
With tentacles that arc and sweep
above my head and in my mind
I know you hold the answers
that somewhere in your silver bark
is food for souls and drink for hearts

I enter now your portal arch
of draped and drawn far-reaching limbs
of shelter from this world of harm
yes. I am here and will not leave
the haven that I sought is found

Closing Time

The monotonic tuneless song
that tells of life and things gone wrong
and blouses with their polka dots
you listen when they are torn off

where dancers bring the drinkers cheer
who laugh and cry into their beer
and fiddlers fiddle till they stop
so men can dance on the polka dots

it groans of naked summer moons
swimming faster not in tune
galloping to its acid end
the rugged handsome singer bends

yet croons of loneliness and love
of damaged hearts and Him above
beating speeding into frenzy
a cry, a sigh, as in a daze he

tells us that it's closing time
that nothing's happening, life's divine
we are left hungry breathless
in the silence that he's left us.

Cracks and All

It's Friday and Project X is no further forward.
It didn't help that you swore at the meeting yesterday.
You, who, in the past, was always so upbeat and helpful — a
      cup runneth over type of person.
It didn't help for a dreamless night either
as you replayed the talks over and over in your head.

But today dawned with a blood-blushed sky
You were hopeful, you know what that always means though
      and you worry for the fishermen out there.
The thrum of the helicopter overhead adds to the worry. The
      not-knowing. You try not to think
about the old wooden Maria-Janie out there lobstering.
You keep busy, but the niggles won't leave you.

The ice is preventing you from going anywhere today.
There is no sand for the paths.
Snowshoes won't help in this. So you throw another log on the
fire and watch the orange glow catch up with the blue from the
flickering flames.

The power is down again too.
It's no wonder you've started swearing at meetings.
But you know that's not really the answer.
You set the old kettle on the wood stove and wait for it to sing.
You hum along with Onward Christian Soldiers before bursting
into Cohen's Anthem, reminding yourself of the great man's
clever lyrics: ...how the light gets in...

And for whatever reason, you feel more positive and remind yourself that what is past is past, that tomorrow is uncertain and what really matters is now. Cracks and all.

da Vinci's Burlington House Cartoon

Saint Anne points to heaven
surely knowing
where her grandson ultimately will go.

She turns to his mother, The Virgin Mary,
as if to say, 'All will be fine.
It is his destiny.'

But what of our destiny? Can she point to that?

Her hand is prominent
different. Added later?
An afterthought?

Or is her hand the essence of the drawing's message?

Following her unblemished finger I see nothing.
But still she points.
Insisting.

I am alone with the cartoon
soaking up, questioning this extraordinary story
executed by the master five hundred years ago.

What did he know?

Oh Leonardo
Why have you brought to me this family?

Of mother daughter son. And cousin?
John the Baptist?
How have you made me think?

Now I've drunk all there is to drink
of this art
overflowing with thought
I drift through the staircases
seeking The National Gallery's tea-room

closer to understanding destiny.

Death Wish

under the smell of thunder
death creeps grey upon the deaf
smile sick honey
tile without words
braille will not help you now

Declaration

If you ask me one more time
I swear I'll...
If you look at me like that
I know I'll...
If you touch me with your gentleness
I feel I'll...
If I smell your summer fragrance
I must...
If I taste your sweet surrender
I will try and...
If I hear you say those words
I'll tell you...

Please help me kiss you back
and look at you with love
Please take my hand in your hand
and drink the scent you crave
Please help me find the words
and listen with your heart
then I will tell you...

Dissection

The time has come to take this thing apart
to analyse and break it down
with hand on scalpel for a pen
to slice and dice for what's within.

What is the time? Is there a clock
to tell the mind to form a thought
with hands that turn around around
pointing numbers as you're taught.

Fingers pointing parts dissecting
words misshapen and misformed.
Do you know the right from wrong
or is what's left the real song?

Reform without the recipe
stitch it back without due care
close your eyes and loosen grips
on pens—just words that cut the edge.

dolmades (i)

One taste. That's all it took, a bite, then chew and swallow.
1960 back at Smokey Joe's. Air is blue, hazed with charred
kebabs. Lazy nights. Mezes with succulent morsels on saucers.
And you.
Across the table.

dolmades (ii)

One taste. that's all it took.
Smokey Joe's 1960.
Mezes with succulent morsels on saucers.
Suck and swallow.
I am back.
The air is blue.
Hazed with charred kebabs.
And you across the table.

Each

Each night she left me with my dinner for one
the TV talkers in the corner of the room
a brief whiff of her disappearing perfume

Each morning she arrived with a brisk 'hello' plumped my
    pillows
changed my channels
brushed my hair
while I drank in her smile

Each afternoon we listened to piano pieces on the radio
together frozen in a past drinking tea
with brown bread and butter and red jam tarts

Those days are gone and she is too
with her faint scents of violets
yellow ribbons in her hair flying
In the wake of tomorrow's breezes.

Emerging Reason

The shadow image draws the game away
along the lines once frayed
but now defined
let us not kid
ourselves
This is not just a game but a time when
good will win the evil bet or better
still erase the red that drapes
across the bed of cotton
white and crisp like
early morning
toothpaste

Unmarked for now
but as the day unfolds
like petunia petals in garden-centre hanging baskets
revealing price tags and exotic names dreamed up by
bouncy energised marketing grads

We will see the truth

Event?

We float away on dim recalls
under bridges over gold wagons
babies grizzle and drizzle sweet mothers' milk
down silk bibs embroidered with dragons

Boats putter and puddle in patterns
frozen in time like old paintings
the grey and the blonde swig their cider
collapsing in joy without parting

But now it is done and all over
boards will come down with the flagpoles
the hoards will go back where they came from
like frogs turning legless to tadpoles

Fly

Fly
Pretty gulls into prisms of light
it's a long way to go
but you'll be there by night
like white shirts in the moonlight
snowflakes at dawn
your strength is your weakness
to carry you on
fly
off you go to fathomless heights
with your feathers of flight
like wisps of silk bright

Fresh Blood

Like cabochons of garnets splashed across a field of snow
or scatterings of petals from a budding Cabot rose
My heart will never beat if I see signs like these again
they mark an end of yearning
when I mourn
another death before
a life is born

The past is full of blood and pain and sorrow
of tiny mites who never had a chance to suck my breast
With leaden heart I laid to rest without their hands to clutch
I live with dread that I should
ever see
fresh crimson blood before
you come to me

Getting Older

As if on air
she walks silently in black
aware without looking at the bandage
sensing without smelling the burning
the ground is remarkably frosted
still. There is no time for reading

The palm reading
could have been written in the air
her mind while stopped becomes frosted
with ominous cloud-like black
memories burning
wanting to unwrap the bandage

Please remove the bandage
she pleads for keys to reading
anguish burning
against thick putrid air
but all she sees is black

Her memories hang like frosted
limpets clinging to bandage
some white some blue some black
like leaves in teacups for reading
some lost like air
wisps of smoke after burning

burning, burning, burning
clearing she feels the frosted
opening in the air
waves licking away the bandage
forgetting much of the reading
remembering before the black

Slowly clouds no longer black
warmly but with no more burning
the thing she forgets is the reading
no longer heated nor frosted
falling away from the bandage
revealing mists in the air

Crisp frosted bandage
burning the readings
calling no black through the air.

Glimpsing a Nova Scotia Autumn

Festivals of apples scarecrows
ukuleles fiddles all
kilts aswirling — celtic colours
that's Cape Breton in the fall.

Everyone is carving pumpkins
faces glowing noses eyes
nothing's wasted in this province
thanksgiving tables groan with pies.

Hiking, biking, boats still sailing
embracing last of fall's warm days
lost in gazing with amazement
at our famous autumn trees:

maples, birches, poplars, oaks
blazing scarlets, russets, golds.

He's Still in the Phone Book

At the bottom of the trunk
a faded brown telephone book
cover torn
yellow corners curled
where tongue-licked fingers
repeatedly sought
short numbers to dial

She could still hear
the grind
of the dial going round

Remembering
like a lighter's flash
shining stars on the toecaps
of his black
polished
shoes
Spit he said
that was the way

She drew the book up to her face
to catch the smell of his pipe
finding instead
tucked between pages
for boat rides and coach outing
his first bus pass
the reason for celebration

A trip around the bay
and back
without getting seasick
won the day.

Hindsight

Is it an age thing?
when days spin into weeks and months and years
and before you know, you are your mother's age
saying the same things
beginning *in my day*
and ending *wait until you're my age*

When did that happen?
that flip to looking back
to hindsight
to wisdom
instead of looking forward
to the unknown
to big plans
to hope

When did you start saying *life is not a dress rehearsal*
to the young wasting their youth before your eyes
as you once did

You ask yourself: if we could rewind
and do it all again
would we do it differently?
how can you answer?

Honestly?
Every moment before this one
made you who you are today

Would you want it any other way?

How You Think You Might Find Happiness

You'll light a giant bonfire. To blaze forever. To feed ad
    infinitum.
To be seen, glowing with many shades of crimson,
gold and emerald,
in the night sky for miles. Will people think it the Aurora?

You salivate anticipating the euphoria.

Resolving to find happiness
armed with gleaming black plastic garbage bags
to clear your life of all that's not essential.

To give you space to breathe.

Dispelling thoughts of potential losses
of possessions once precious
of letting go of your life on paper
in yellowing mountains of dust filled files
of portfolios of disintegrating pastel portraits. From an era long
    gone.

You waver before heaping into garbage bags
your shelves of baby photos
wondering: will it feel like losing your babies
burning your babies?

Late in the city night
watching sparks fly. Like fireflies into the violet skies,
reaching the heavens, shooting you achievements
and your paper babies into the hereafter.
the bonfire's tongues engulfing bags brimming with surplus
        chattels
exploding into the unknown. Into nothingness.

In the cold light of day
more excess miscellany
more gleaming black plastic garbage bags
more continual feeding of flames

knowing you're exchanging memorabilia for memories
in your new found breathing space.

I am

I am the island
Floating reflections in wells drawn by blindfold donkeys
where St. Paul once walked.

I am aroma memories of Smokey Joe's late night feasts
tinkling laughter clinking glasses upside down on
       handkerchiefs
on Father's head. For dancing.

I am snatches of language yassou file mou.
On my tongue lemon soup with wild garlic. A freshening
       spring
in the green Morris Minor to the foothills of Kantara

I am not the Roman tile once picked up from ruins
to become a teapot stand. That was Mother,
who had bad luck so took it back to Salamis

I am the fear of moustachioed Eoka gathering
firearms lining the Coca Cola walls in Akhna's cafe
the day I missed the bus

I am the evacuee who sailed away
across the Mediterranean from my golden island's sun
to dreary grey safety

I was this place. This taste. This light. This tongue.
Those herbs. Those songs. Those nights.
That time. That understanding. That feeling.

I am.

If only

If only they'd each been content with their lot.
If only he hadn't told her in the first place.
If only she hadn't bothered to listen.
If only he hadn't bought her a drink.
If only she'd said, 'no thanks.'
If only he hadn't made the suggestion.
If only she hadn't offered to switch.
If only the weather had been fine.
If only she'd had her brakes checked.
If only he hadn't been on the phone.
If only it was Thursday not Wednesday.
If only he'd had a good night's sleep.

Into the light

For Julia

Fifty-five years old
after more than twenty
years with multiple sclerosis
black tunnels without light or hope

Along comes a tiny ray of possibility
threaded with life changing
solutions building to real
ways forward bursting
into the light as an

Independent

Woman

It's Worth Mentioning

It's worth mentioning the drawing board is not something to
    get back to
but to move onward with its well-worn rounded blackened
    corners
ridges grooved where clips once held the newsprint
on which you sketched the ten-second gesture figures moving
across the scene like ghosts of an age when every day was
a day with charcoal in hand and on your hands
fingerprinting walls and doors
as you stopped to make a cuppa

It's worth mentioning the purple bicycle is not looking to be
    pedalled
again but again wouldn't pink petunias look good
in its wicker basket that you bought spontaneously when on
    holiday
squeezing it into your suitcase to take home across the Atlantic
where you could have bought an Indian-woven basket without
the challenge of transporting it to another world for another
    bicycle
that once had three wheels (a tricycle then) and a boot for your
    six-year-old rocks

It's now worth mentioning the red sports car that had no room
    for children
they squeezed onto the parcel shelf but loved it anyway
map reading the way out of Southampton to the west country
    with

great skill at six-years-old when being given responsibility is a
    wonderful thing
after sailing in a banana boat from Bermuda

It should be worth mentioning of course
that some of this is long forgotten
returning in fragmented flashes of oil paints' odours
and of Mother's 4711 eau de cologne
subtle fragrances of Albertine roses climbing round the front
    door
tastes of pomegranates picked out with pins
lychees from the gnarled tree in the front garden all sand and
    dust
and pungent Rogan Josh at a time when heartburn
was not worth mentioning

glimpses of decades

Is it worth mentioning that moving onward is the only option
with wisdom of hindsight (what is that?)?
If it is the should-haves and could-haves then what might have
been would have been sans charcoal sketching and purple
    bicycles
no wicker baskets nor pink petunias
nor red sports cars with squished but happy kiddies
And fragmented memories would have been
Scentless and flavour less.

It was worth mentioning, wasn't it?

Journey to a World Away

A wish
Drifts down on chiffon wings of dragonflies
Before your eyes

On a salver
Like a rondel's slivers of silken carpets
A thought

In your mind
Mingling with tempting juices of apricots and honey
In a flute

For your tongue
To taste in sips of life — a distant world of exotic
Dance and music

For your ears
Discordant yet alluring as your fingers flex and flicker
To the flame

To reach and touch
And hold the realness of another's life in a world away
In wishes

Killer

The porcupine killed the
Austrian Pine, working
slowly, peeling bark, day after
day, branch after branch, until
the tree stripped bare,
blanched, naked to the world,
bled to death.

Lament for Nelly

Run free sweet Nell
'cross sands and fields
And far off distant hills.
You've tasted honey
Lain your weary racing bones
On plump soft beds off foam

Have fun young Nell
This was no place for the old.
So take flight. Take fancy
The open road is yours now
While in our hearts and minds
Here you'll always be. Nelly.

Nelly, AKA Manna Rocky Top, racing greyhound extraordinaire.
February 25th, 2003 - December 24th, 2012

Lament for the Future

Led sings of a stairway to heaven
as I lie back to back with the world
I want to step up but can't find the plate
so I stay in my foetal curl

Van sings of forests and waterfalls
as I sink down in my abyss
I want to go home but can't find the road
for the woods stink thicker than piss

Pete's death on the stairs goes nowhere
as my ears swallow lyrics of ghosts
my head tells me no, nor one step at a time
my arms stretch full out for the host

It's Teddy Bears' Picnic for morons
darting bluebells are no longer blue
I'll tiptoe through life fucking tulips
leave the mess of the rest up to you

Last Song for George

Soft and gentle voice
each sweet note
tells of a time
now gone

Song of then, but now and when
no syllable of
lyric is lost
in noise

Four strings of innocence
speak for the world
as rose petals fall
with our tears

On each word we bow
in honour as the
melody says
it all

Life

Sitting by the window watching plants grow in the sun
makes me think of life and the road it took me on
I look back on my childhood many years ago
so simple and carefree like a tune on a banjo

My road gets murky then like trails of dust sometimes
decisions made or falterings besmirched by tiring climbs
but wheels kept turning on and up until I reached the top
there was no sign of a dead end and no-one shouted stop

I fell into the usual traps of marriage work and kids
round and round the hamster wheel as years slid by on skids
and then one morning, like today, I woke and felt the sun
and told myself, get out there girl it's time you had some fun

My eyes were opened at that point, no forks in roads to take
the lane of life was in my grasp, the cake was mine to bake
I'm at the starting line once more, carefree but more wise
I know the route, the bends, the turns, I also see the skies

And feel the sand between my toes, the water lapping sweet
abandoned shoes and cotton socks, I feel life through my feet
it is a path without a road, without the need for wheels
I've learned to stop, not yearn for more

Yes, this is how it feels

Light Bulb Moment

Bus stop
Ferry hop
Bands playing
Nerves jarring
Waters lapping
Distant sightings
Memory racking
Fingers tapping
Realisation
Déjà vu

Line Up

the bronze is done
the line is set in standing somnolence
shuffling slowly slumping forward
towards
the future

or the past
petrified persons placed by
numbers counting hours never
ever
minutes

installation art
expressing times of horror
booed and mocked by those within
will win
The Turner Prize

Making up the Numbers

The party invitation hits with a thud
to refuse would be rude
to attend a nightmare
but
I must go
you never know

Always the mouse
on the outside looking in
never in the spotlight
God forbid
drawing anyone's attention

Alone in the kitchen
left out of laughter, music
dancing, love
only dirty glasses and forks
for company
as always

Teeth gritted between red
gashed lips
I grab my coat and
go home
alone

Man in a bar

Well may you sit with your melancholy
looking into the abyss of an erstwhile life
while Missy in the bright white shirt
looks on

She pours wine and looks you in the eye
you do not see the bottle, the glass, the lass
you seek the past within the darkness
looking back

There is no future for you in full bodied
bulls' blood wine — but a hankering for goulash
wafts then drifts on by with other tastes of consciousness
Searching now

For somehow you'll remember days when
you sat around a checkered table sipping
bread-scooping that rich herb scented gravy
for your love

You stand and tip the white shirt girl
smile and offer thanks for succour
that took you through the gloom and out into
the place you need to be.

Marriage Vows

If I could see you
through this blindfold
tethered as I am to drowning
in the flashing lights

If you promise
not to blow away
like old and folded paper
when I empty
out my handbag
in the street
for all
to
run and
catch
the
remnants of my life
listed in supermarket
receipts
and shopping lists
of Terry's Chocolate Oranges
and custard tarts

Then I promise you
I will stay
until we're
swept away
together

Mauritius Roadside Chili Cakes

1.
You smell them long before you reach
the roadside vendors
with their Creole chants
vus'ashette, vus'ashette très sho, très bon
(you buy you buy very hot very good)
as they pile more coals on their glowing brasiers

2.
The air is thick with smoke and spice
intoxicating, tantalising, choking
but then the sprit and crackle
as the pallid hand-formed dough patties
filled with mysteries from exotic soils
are lowered into the encrusted mesh basket
into the dark as treacle boiling oil

3.
Turning golden before your closing eyes
breathing deeply the aroma
tasting foreign
burning fingers
tossing from hand to hand
blowing to cool
then the first wetly anticipated nibble
before
teeth receive the empyreal bite
and tongue gets its reward.

Mother Nature Speaks

Look up and see the spaces in between
of cerulean unknown heights
beyond the gnarled and stunted
by the human trimming

Once so strong and tall

Move to your left and see the spaces in between
the shift to mackerel skies
beyond the dark and battered
by the human beatings

Once so strong and tall

Turn around and see the spaces left behind
cluttered with crowded dwellings
beneath what should be arms
of nature's protection

Once so strong and tall

Are they all gone now?
is there a chance to bring back
the da Vinci genius tree theory?
That they will stand strong and tall once more?

Moving On

In the clearing of the clutter from my muddled brain
I see a future without blemishes
of battles that boil like summer in the city
crevassed horizon dividing any harmony between us

It is time to turn a page in our lives
to say goodbye to a past of irritating anger
that simmers like haze in a desert
instead remember the good times

If this is the way it ends, so be it
there will be no last-minute change of mind
no looking back over shoulders but
reaching forward, looking up and moving on.

Music of Life

Rachmaninoff surges through Brief Encounter
arpeggios run to climaxes and you hold your breath
smelling that cold railway station coffee
in what would be the defining moment for them.

You dream of feeling connected between music
and life, but this now-life of social networking
texting and unreal reality TV
holds no defining moments for you.

Then you find that like a good old London bus
there is a higher level from which you may
view the world
watch life through soft-lighted windows
with open curtains and with each embrace
with each scowl
with each tear and laugh
you will hear
Rachmaninoff's piano concerto rise beyond the first climax
Cohen growling Hallelujah
The Bare Naked Ladies rock If I had a Million Dollars
and a thousand voices rise in harmony with Zadoc the Priest

My Grandmother

If I had a quarter of Nuttall's Mintoes I could turn into my grandmother and suck and chew the lot while waiting for Mrs Dale's Diary to start on the wireless.

If I had net curtains I could turn into my grandmother and tweak them while waiting for him to come home.

If I had a round rosewood table with curly legs I could turn into my grandmother and walk around and around waiting, watching his supper grow cold.

If I had my grandmother now I could ask her why she spent her life waiting.

Not Fade Away

It's so easy to relive the day
I heard the news
to feel the loss of something
I barely had the chance to love

I feel it now
the overflow of teenage
emotions forty-four years ago
like yesterday

Yet every day your voice
gets a little closer
as it fills my ageing heart with ballads
of a time once loved

Oh Boy
I hear you sing
early in the morning
and I feel my heart beat as a thousand drums
it's so easy to remember
the day when it was
raining in my heart

Ode to a Nova Scotia Spring

It is your time to rouse this sleeping earth
from frozen lands where nothing seemed to live
for months: blanched wilderness of icy dearth
while silently beneath it all you give
us hope, as overnight bright furled ferns break
green fiddleheads through monochromic loam.
Pussy willows shake silver buds awake
the bluets by the melting brook to bloom.

Your forest floor turns amber and burnt umber
then fragile haze of grass and fresh new growth
with speedwell spears rising from their slumber
while ivy vines worm through thick undergrowth.
Maple boughs are bare but bear the promise:
rising sap with syrup for arrivals
of yellow-bellied birds to peck and kiss
the bark with drills for their young's survival.

Peeping frogs sing of the season's op'ning
raucous in their, oh so welcome, chorus.
Woodlands come alive with chipmunks darting,
chattering like children on the school bus.
Nesting in hollow trees are chickadees
a lone hawk watches — waits — hovers on wing.
Wild bees, gold-heavy from the pis-en-lit
confirms your season: fresh and fragrant spring.

on a beach walk August 2011

It's times like this you realise how blessed you are
while the civilised world riots for its causes
you answer to the call of the shore's wild curlews

And pause

Not a footprint in the sand ahead and not a cloud to mar the
        sky
you allow nature's repeating ocean roar to beat in time with your
mind
confirming with more than a glimmer that still there are slivers

Of peace

That not all society burns with anger that some pick up the ash
and debris and from the heart-searching truth emerges
A new generation and it's times like this you realise the answers

Are there.

Once

I shut my eyes and see between the dotted grackles
a land that once was green and luscious
now devoid of anything but worms
and parked cars

I close my lips and taste the air between the clouds
a flavour once so sweet and filled with juice
now dried as prunes in packets
from supermarkets

I cover my ears and hear the drone between my hands
of industry and commerce before it slows
and grinds to a stilted fundless
halted starkness

I clench my fist but still I feel the silvery touch
of pure clean water from the stream
before man's poison left its
pockmarked mess

I block my nose but still I smell wild roses that once grew
in hedgerows and in banks before the meadow
became a building site where nothing
lives in darkness

One more time

The sunken sound of broken bells
clashing their distant rumble
reminding us there once was a time
telling us: be humble

The morning frost midst crunching needles
from tall strong pines
reminding us there's still more time
telling us: to shine

All dust and feathers in our heads
brushing up our minds
reminding us there has to be
at least: just one more time

Only O?

Symphony of clowns
forty wolf moons flock
sword down frowns of sorry

Scotch cold pops clock
from tops of rocks
roll mops bowls of worry

Oh how slops stop
psycho's cyclops
short thorn morn nor mossy

box for brown dog's
trophy — ghost frogs'
dodgy sons torch stormy

long worms stock
droopy short sloths
throw floss on lost gold lorry

Symphony forty sword
Scotch from roll
Oh psycho's short
box trophy dodgy
Long droopy throw floss
Found the lost 'O'.

Pairings

Passionfruit and peppermint
Artichoke with apricot
Endives with blackberries
Brie with a dram of whisky

Sea urchin and kiwi fruit
Pawpaw with fresh parmesan
Coconut with crispy bacon
Shiitake with Peking duck

Kumquat with cardamom
Dry gin and aubergine
Parsley and strong black tea
Greek honey with sardines

Papua dark chocolate
With buttermilk or peas
Boiled eggs with cauliflower
Perfect couplings these

Patterns

Patterns of life
blocked or
tissue
paper pinned and sheared around
marked for seams
notched for darts

In temporary homes
cardboard boxes with constant
shifting sounds like
crackles of crisp packets
impossible to walk
in silence
with over-bent backbones
like cumulus clouds

papuros

of paper birds
that rustle
with the breezes
and songs they bring

of paper flight
caught in hand
and eye and heart
that you may sing

of paper girls
claiming all
the love I have
feeling their sting

of paper smile
beating now
on fickle frown
o paper wing

Point of View

You stand at three feet recommended for viewing
but you can't grasp the message so you move back to eight

Others around you whisper and snigger
they don't bother to stop
like you
rooted

Red swirls your mind it plays with your head
with misleading splashes of alizarin crimsons and vermillion

Judging you
judging the painting
is it sky?
What gives you the right
to make sense of what first appears
to be nonsense

Cadmium and chrome yellows
battle for dominance
in three-sided
lop-sided
five-sided
elements
tumbled and jumbled

until

Strong lines draw you
in
to the
cobalt blue
vortex

And still
the eye
in the corner

watches you

Postcard from The Western Isles

We've reached this land that once was theirs
to kneel, to touch our forebears' earth,
taste salt of sea-thrown island air.
We feel this land which once was theirs
before cruel lairds declared them, 'Clear
from crofts, your lives, your place of birth.'

We found this land that once was theirs.
We've knelt and kissed our forebears' earth.

Postcard (for Ma) from Cape Breton

Ma — walking in the footsteps of our kin
who landed on these shores in 1810:
crofters cleared out from their highland homes
leaving all behind they've ever known
to start their lives again.

Ma — see the map? The place marked with a pin?
That's Iona, the place that guards within
those crofters' names and from whence they came,
to start their lives again.

Ma — this became New Scotland to these men
and women who, by Bras d'Or lakes or in
harsh fields, skirled their pipes and kept their songs,
swirled their kilts and worked to right the wrongs
discharged upon them back in 1810.
To start their lives again.

Postcard from Prince Edward Island

wide skies kiss red sands
at Green Gables, fabled home
of spirited Anne

Rameau's Menuet en Rondeau

Rameau's Menuet en Rondeau
for piano
With dancing hands
On keys of gleaming Steinway Grands
Mezzo forte
hear the glory,
pianissimo to gentle
accidentals.
Unrivalled — swift —
that's Rameau's gift.

Reading a Poem Before Breakfast

I read a poem called Orange Peel* early today
it wasn't really about orange peel
but about cleaning up garbage

The title of the poem left me
with an image in my mind
of scented pores and pockmarked skin
that's always described as
orange peel

I read the poem three times
each time my senses returning to the title
Orange Peel
I could taste anticipation of sweetness
of pulpy juices from blood oranges
the peel landing over my shoulder
with the initial
of my lover
to be

That's not really about orange peel
either
is it?
But about dreams and hopes that someone whose name begins
    with 'S'
(why does the orange peel always land with an 'S'?
will dance to me on a mystic white charger.
Will he be a Stan or Simon or Steve?

I'll take the orange pips and plant with hope
and water well with this young girl's dreams
of walking through my orange grove
with Stan or Simon or Steve.

The poem, Orange Peel, is by John Milton Hayes

Reflection

The lake is flat-ass calm today
a different scene from
last night's raging storm
when tall trees creaked and groaned
the mountains cracked and moaned
the rains beat down and washed our words away

The truth: all that remains is clear
we see life's multitudes
of near and distant views
one moment wild and furious
the next a mirror smooth with glory
is that what we can really love or fear?

The lake will never hold the answers
nor distant towering hills
or winds or rains that chill
we'll learn to take them all
and wonder
so we may each find the perfect partner
then you and I can be the leading
dancers

Rejection

On a pedestal I poise
or a black velvet chaise
I languish
basking
in your mouthings of promises

In your bed I spread
and curl
soaking
your devotion and worship
wanting nothing more

now the hollow emptiness
surrounding
less than everything
I would prefer
not knowing love at all

wandering
for wanting
seeking something more
sleeping in each archway
all with bolted doors

Resilience

Crisis caused the unexpected change of heart
upon his purple pockmarked face turning aside
had he lost all respect?

Surrendered now, tired, at least she tried
inquired until exhausted, no fight left
wearily she rose
which window to look out? She preferred
and chose the double glazed.

Gazed, catching breath from sobbing, sighing
with the knowledge that she'd quenched it in the bud.

River (i)

Eddying, swirling
Carry my thoughts
Like foaming effervescent
Morsels of anger
And love

Are you slimy?
You have the look of silk
A dark grey menace
to wrap around
my shoulders

And on your travels
With me astride
I hold my breath
In grief

Until
I feel the life let go
I float
I soar
To freedom
Like a bird

River (ii)

murky, mystery
holding secrets in depths of
mud sludge detritus

grey skies preventing
reflections of blue heaven
without butterflies

no wind to ruffle
brown river waters feathers
of bird song long gone

River (iii)

The moon's riding high, this night of all nights
When every line on your palm speaks of danger
With stillness you move
As if without breath
With no fear of alarm or of anger

Life's written in starlight reflected in glass
While shifting through fields of destruction
Finding the way
As only you can
Just one world away from the ocean.

Sandscript

Twisting turning like a tangled ball of wool
the intricate pattern woven by worms
at the water's edge holds messages
for those who care to stop

and read the words upon the sands
clear untangled lines
with answers to the threads of
ravelled disconnects

The tide will take them twice each day
and leave behind unblemished
untrod clean and wordless
sands ready to begin
anew

Seize the Day

Do you have the will to fly
to take your eyes to fresh new worlds
the shape of which you've never felt
or seen?

Does your sun and moon still turn
or does your day pull through in drags
never ceasing nor delighting? Does
it hurt?

Open up your arms and soar
where they will take you do not fear
the unknown mountains vales and oceans
of life.

If you give, it's yours for taking
circulating laughter and your love
sharing all the sadness and the joy
like food.

Signals

don't look for signals
from my shoulders
as they drop or rise with how I
feel

today or even yesterday the signs
of failure or success can
be in simple body
language

speaking arms on screens with clouds
of tomorrow's signs of rain
or sun or ice and snow
fall

from my eyes you'll read
much more than waving arms
and shoulders' slumps or
raises

see now the sadness and the joy
of time ahead with which
to live with all you can
give.

Sister of No Mercy

Between the lines
not so young when
you taught fear and cowering —
I learned tough and unbelieving.
Whatever Leonard says
I say he's wrong and hasn't
felt your rod to save this child from spoil.
Sweet smile encased in white
belies the truth
of brown beer bottles
in secret cupboards
waiting for the time
when all us girls
asleep in dorms
liberate you to
more sins

Originally published in Leonard Cohen You're Our Man - 75 poets reflecting on the poetry of Leonard Cohen 2009

She

She stops to watch the firefly
summer's herald in the night
knowing she'll be out of time
as August beckons like a wall
of holes

She walks the river's banks at dark
backwards reading distant lights
of others' futures she has none
no hope of gold days running on
the edge

She turns her back for one last time
a picture freezes on her mind
of dancing fireflies in the sun
impossible to see she walks
alone

Solas

1.
Bright lights and shifting shadows
of blurbs and envirofriendly coils
flickering red and yellow candles on frosted cakes for birthdays
illuminate eager faces flushed with delight
one forced puff and they're gone leaving behind that familiar
    tell-tale smell

2.
Night driving wet black roads like fresh liquorice twists
and turns through cities with giant orange halos fizzing
from villages with star-lit skies to nowhere
at the top of the world the Aurora Borealis emits photons
shooting green and red moving curtains for the dance of the
    spirits

3.
'Let there be light' said the voice

Fesnell heard
so ships could pass in the night
looking for home finding the light to save souls

Edison Swan and Davy heard
Emitting inspirations of incandescence
on drawing boards

Potts heard

so the flow would stop and go from red to amber then to green
headlights flashing car horns crashing impatient fathers
        leaving home

Einstein heard
with meters telling of exposure for lambency recording for all
        time
actinically secret images of what has gone before

Blaisdell heard
so Zippos would be there for Marlena, 'Have you gotta light
boy?' Scarlet talons flicking cigarette holder made in jade
        while lipsticked lips turn blue with cold

Gould heard
as did others with their lasers
fighting with light sabres to claim their prize

And there was light.

Something Special

There was something in the songs he wrote
something in the resonant
something in the memorable
the messages were strong
but even deeper now

George sang of Something
in the way his lover moved
and in her smile
he didn't want to leave her
now or ever

But leave he did.

After sadness
Celebration
Music
Song

Joe sang of happiness that used to be
rose petals fell on the hush of thousands
softly joining the final anthem
of tender eyes shining
lighting the way

Seeing him in our dreams

Taking the Zig-Zag Ferry in Nineteen Seventy Something

I zig-zagged the Bosporous
The Istanbul Strait
From Europe to Asia and back
                                Dancing the floors of the
                                      Chicken soup waters
                                Each port of call offering a snap
Landscape of living through
Coffee and yoghurt
Or goats as they boarded the boat
                                The Black Sea approaching
                                   Yoros Kalesi towering
                                With gun-toting soldiers aloft
The long day behind me
Returned to Galata
The moon biggest I'd ever seen
                                          As I pen this account
                                      I smell diesel, rice pudding
                                    Foods of old Turkey's delight
The calls are now wailing
The faithful are bowing
And foreign tongues churn through the night
                                              Rich spices linger
                                      Drifts through my memory
                                    History sifts through my mind

Tea Party Madness

Heads float bobbing in teacups, wetted hair waiting for silver spoons stirring from sickly stupor, lifting limbs and dipping saucers swallows sighs darts departing? Drinks the turgid tea regardless.

Tell your children to

stare if they like
to gather those images
fill up with light
if there's nobody there
at the house on the
corner
questions unspoken
unheard
unanswered

A gambling man told me
to keep a straight face
to look dead ahead
not a hair out of place
you may appear crazy
but leave it unspoken
unheard
unanswered

That's couples for you

She dearly wished for a new three-piece suite with loose covers,
washable, cream with blush-pink roses and leaves the colour of
    emeralds

He'd set his heart on a new three-piece suit in navy and white
    pinstripes
with matching waistcoat, a pocket for his gold watch and chain

She sometimes thought about telling him of her wishes, pulling
at the loose threads of the coarse bark brown of the old settee
but saying nothing

He often hinted about going to the races — not having
    anything to wear
plucking at his corduroys as if they were riddled with fleas then
    picking up his paper

She told no one, at the furniture shop she chose the rose-
    covered covers
ordered the new suite on the never-never something they swore
they'd never do

He hung his new suit in the garden shed so she wouldn't see
slinking off down the garden path to the races
with no gold watch for his pocket

The new suite arrived in a very large van.
The old was removed.
She hovered in nervous joy.

He watched her with unspoken love
and disappeared into the garden shed
emerging in his navy three-piece suit.

"If only you'd said," they said in unison.
Holding hands.
Sitting on the blush-pink roses with emerald leaves.

The Cookery Book Given to You by Your Mother

The book, given years ago by Mother
with yellowed pages, curling corners marked
'how to bake a cake to net your lover'

answers 'tween the blue/grey linen covers?
are recipes for love affairs of hearts
in the book you've had for years from Mother

Take a large bowl — crack six eggs of plovers
but careful now for here's the tricky part
in how to bake good cakes that capture lovers

You add another message above hers
'add honey to the cherries or they're tart'
in the cookbook given by your mother

Now rest a while then you will discover
the secrets hidden in your mother's charts:
how to bake a cake to keep your lover

pages safe between those linen covers
tell so much more than recipes impart
the book given years ago by mother:
how to bake a cake to love your lover.

The day my grandfather drowned the kittens

The ripples of the draining board
leave dimples on my bum
my grubby knees are scrubbed
until the garden dirt is gone
the itch remains and memories
of kittens facing death
I hear their mewing cries
until they take their final breath

Beneath the rosewood table
with its bulging bulbous legs
behind the chenille cloth
with its tassels tied in knots
I hear them speak about me
as if I am not there
I see their frowns in stipples
through the fringes of my hair

He lifts his pipe with steady
easy puffs and reads the paper
she chews her Lovell's Mintoes
while looking through the window
I know without them saying
that I'm changed from this ordeal
they dry my tears with promise
that I'll live and time will heal.

The fall at the waterfalls

the force and roar, the churn and draw
she had no way to tell its power
in bright red hoodie and big sunglasses
she climbed the barrier for

her perfect pose for the classic photo
holds umbrella aloft while the waters below
rush the Horseshoe Falls at Niagara
she gives a Kodak smile and a flirty flash

one slip and she's gone, carried away
in that force and that roar
the falls overpower her
screams unheard as the water takes her

a 19-year-old Japanese student was swept over the Horseshoe Falls, Niagara, Ontario on 14th August 2011. At time of writing, her body had not been found.

The Feel of Dark

1
Nanny I can't see
my young mewls cry through the night
she calls back
You'll have to feel like they do in France

Grasping the edges of the eiderdown
stitched in pink like raspberries
five-year-old fingers reaching for ridges
of peeling treacle Anaglypta

not hearing her grandmotherly smile

All I knew about France back then:
Grandpa was there in his youth
a Hussar with a horse-pulling gun carriage
fighting in brown sticky mud

the darkest of times

2
I can't see
my mind's eyes watch voices
telling me
Come back to us, don't go, all will be okay

Seeking his hand through the dark
his finding mine cold as glass

50-year-old fingers reaching for living
his rough tanned, strong in perfection

holding my reply

I know about darkness
caught on the cusp of the spiral of shell ice
sucked by the easy lightness of death
love pulling back to the blackness that's life

tip-touching the dark

3
I can see now
there's no-one to hear me cackling with laughter
at my grandmother's old adult joke
of touchy French feeling

Rolling naked in stitches on sheepskins
in warm prancing firelight
70-year-old fingers trace images
of once vanished memories

feeling the dark

The Ghost Writer

Swiftly now before the dawn
Creeps into this final day
Scribe, describe while he sleeps
Make the plot come alive.

Those character who have no soul
Become your own, just for a while
They leap and love, they hate and kill
While he slumbers on without a care

Grey settings damp and with no fire
You work so they abound with colour
Life and smell or living hell
It matters not
It's just your job

To be in someone else's head
While he luxuriates in bed
You close the file with no regret

The last eclipse

Languishing in an outdoor hot tub
on the slopes of California's grass valley
is an old man sucking a cigar stub
not waiting in the dark but

staring at the moon's full light
and the blue black Pacific tipped in ruffled
ripples of gold and gleaming white
not hearing nature's expectancy

the old man waits for the eclipse
sips and clinks his highball ice
with warming whisky on his lips
not knowing this will be his last

in a lifetime's memories that fade
as earth's dark shadows brings the dark
to the lunar sky
while quiet invades

not feeling, the old man closes his eyes.

The Loss of Rosalind

It is the sound, the voice of night
that churns the corners of his mind
to keep from sleep
to drench with wake
and pulse with ice
each limb, each bone, each vein.

At dawn the night is drawn
away in threads but still
his heart is left in shreds.
This light is not for him
without her warmth, her love.

He wills his eyes to close
in sleep
with hopes to dream
of Rosalind.

The Midnight Bus

The late night bus humdrums through dim-lit
yellow streets
with yobbos calling names
to kids in hockey jerseys black
on red

Tells me it's that time of year when
sultry evenings watching darting fireflies
gazing
over phosphorescent bays
are over

Console ourselves with hopes to come
of warm wood stoves and wool blankets
and cease to hanker for
what's past

The Push

Remember the wildflower garden
where we walked in the heat of the night
reflecting on life at the edge of the lake
you circling my mind with your words?

The ribbons so white in the dead of the night
were lost when the dawn lastly came
don't fool yourself that I'm so taken in
with daisies and dead violins

Your words are as worthless as limp graveyard flowers
drooping in need of more life
so remember that night in the heat without rain
when your words dripped and died on the ground

The Ravine

We are the rapids rushing
rolling through the gorge
hurtling to the future
in a broiling blue furore
of unstoppable torment

we are the trees watching over you
clawing hanging from the cliffs
and precipices
on rooted threads
and hope and thirst

We are the sheer-faced
granite rocks and slabs
rigid and reliable
encasing your turbulent torrents
watching you go

The reading of the will

(with sincere apologies to H.W. Longfellow)

From her red lips comes a statement,
Aimed into the family group
Never thinking as with always
Ginnie Parker thinks it's hers?
And the law man, bending forward
Pointing finger at the parchment
Tracing signature of witness
Saying to her, "It's not yours."

Through the window sees a sparrow
Flitting down among the leaves
Ginnie mouths her words in silence
"Sorry" shapes but no-one hears.
Takes a pen and strikes through boldly
Says the law man, "All okay?"
For your kinsman it's a godsend
Sorry that it's not your day.

Now the others all sit up straight
Take the wool out of their ears
Listen sharply to the law man
Wonder if it will be theirs
Glance around at uncles, cousins
Till their guts are almost bust
Little Henry half in slumber
Tiny thumb in mouth he sucks.

Henry's daddy can't believe it
When the words are truly read
Henry's mummy, blue eyes smiling
Tells her baby, "It's the best
You're the one who Great Aunt Dora
Thought should have the princely sum."
Ginnie Parker puts her tongue out
uncles, cousins yell, "Not us?"

"It's his windfall," says the law man,
"Let young Henry pave his way
For a future he would not have
Without old Dora's final say."

The Ridgeway – the Oldest Road

Chalk
rolling downland
wide skies
skylarks dart
beech copses
signs of ritual

Ley lines to Uffington
white horses carved
scarps to
valleys
Avebury's circle of stones
cathedrals of time
touching
layers years of warmth
Long Barrow at Kennet

And on to Barbury
Iron Age hill fort
seven white horses
under hooves of grazing sheep
where once King Alfred
stood in victory?

Take the oldest road
but leave
its gentle mysteries
in the windswept landscape.

The Song in Your Head

The song was written in the sun
in trailing words upon the sands
telling of the years now gone
of lovers lost in nature's dance

It travels through the decades as
a train will shudder through its stops
slowing for the bend of words
then speeding for the midnight clock

It is a song that works for all
that speaks of hope or long lost dreams
with choruses predictable
of cadence soaked in melodies

You hear it now as you did when
he danced you to the water's edge
you see his face as you did then
and left you wondering what went wrong

The words will haunt you without end
the tune will trickle through your brain
it will not leave as he once did
that song you both sang in the sun.

The Thinker

A block of stone
with veins
he feels counting ridges
cherishing the threads of time
he taps
gently
and waits for the stone to echo back

It is time
the sculptor picks up his chisel
and carves
the answer

Third Space Inhabitant (A Sense of Place and Home)

A tongue, if it could, would speak in any language. For a fractioned being, parts in different cultures, the past is another country. Unearthed. Deep. Distant. The present is here, spoons banging on coffee cups. The heart knows how to respond.

A body finds love. Love for a place and those who inhabit. No tongues or language needed. The whole has segments. Composed of fragments. They are the slivers of memories darting. Dashing. Seeking out. Clashing and colliding from place to place. Shifting. Settling. Accepting nurture. Shining through this space like the translucent damselfly.

For now.

Dedicated to the memory of Alf and Rena who managed to make things work

Thoughts from the top of the stairs

There is a suitcase in the basement
put there when you went away
I've never opened
never wanted
the scent
of you
again

The hammering, no, more like battering of
words you swung like steel beams
they gleamed and grazed
my speechless mouth
aghast amazed
at what you
had to
say

I will not exit at the next junction
but climb the stronger course
as this cold March night
shifts to early dawn
streaked with
hope I think
I'll throw
you

and your suitcase away

Tick Tock

Tick Tock 1.

"Too little, too late."
"If only we'd known,"
"Is there nothing more we can do?"
"To save ourselves and the planet too?
Or do we have to sacrifice one now? For the other?"

Remember how it was before
when you burned the grass in spring
dead and pale as corn
from the winter's ravages.

You stood with spades and forks
water hoses lest the fires got out of hand.
In early summer new vibrant grass grew
over the scorched earth.

Tick Tock 2.

Committees in cities around tables
banned burning:
"Think of the ozone,"
"Consider the black holes,"
"Protect the planet,"
they yelled across gleaming mahogany board-room tables.
plastic water bottles in one hand. Tablets in the other.
Cellphones in the other.

Three-handed monsters

Tick Tock 3.

Country folk stopped spring rituals
old men chuntered
didn't fancy fines, or jail.
Wild animals continued to cross borders
They'd done it for centuries.
carrying passengers who'd never done any harm.

Before now.

Tick Tock 4.

"Ticks will rule the world
They'll destroy us all.
With their antibiotic-resistant diseases.
Glenda and Frank down the road.
Gone after their bites
by black-legged ticks."

"It's nothing," Frank had said, "just a bite."
Dabbing whisky.
On bullseyes
More whisky for Glenda's.

No dogs or cats or rabbits
For four years
"Do you remember a dog's bark?
Or a cat's purr?"

Tick Tock 5.

Dressed in white from head to toe
To spot the little bastards.
A white population. The law.
No colour left in this world
apart from jewelled green grass sparkling with white intelligent
 ticks.

Never mind the lunatic politicians.
Never mind terrorism.
The ticks are the terrorists.
Helpless scientists with no solutions.
 Epidemics of diseases
carried by insignificant insects:
poppy seed small.

Politicians knew:
legalising cannabis
creating a docile population

***

You know the dosage to overcome
The burning fevers
Blinding headaches
Joint agony muscle loss —

to just let go the fight

So dress in your favourite bright
scarlets and fuchsias
purples and marigolds

lie together on tick-laden grass
watch the sky turn from a blue hue to violet
and drift into oblivion.

Travel this shore with me

In the trail of white-tailed deer
to the pool where gaspereau thrive
there to watch the osprey soar
gliding over swamps and forests
waiting for the time to dive

Pathways beaten by the wild
lead us on up to the drumlin
where we'll scan the land below
sleeping through the sultry weather
gently stirring, distant rumbling

To the shore where Hell Bay breaks
ocean crashes, sea in torment
too rough for snipes and plovers
long grass shelters them from harm
we leave to catch the loons' lament

At Doliver Lake on the old post road
arriving as the sun goes down
waters gilded blazing bronze.

Do you hear the loon's full call?

Tuesday Morning

What do we know of sunshine
if we rarely stop to feel
the golden warmth of friendship
or see smiles on strangers' lips?

What do we know of starlight
if we close our eyes to love
and stumble through long nights alone
wishing for the moon?

What do we know of breaking hearts
if we never take a chance
to feel the beating of the drum
when stars collide with golden sun

It's time to cease reflecting
to go and seize the days
to live them for the gifts they are
to look above at every star
to look around at every smile
and feel the music of our hearts.

Twenty-four Hours of Canadian Winter

At six a.m. on ninety-three point five
forecasters warn of twenty-five below
you wonder, yet again, if you'll survive
from shovelling two metres of fresh snow
or if, by ten past four, your pipes will freeze.
Three dogs must keep you warm throughout the night
iced curlicues of fragile filigrees
on six-paned windows, nature's art. Delight.
On ninety-three point five the following dawn
'today will see a rise to four degrees.'
You leap. Three dogs bound. Time to greet the sun
fling wide those windows, welcome in the breeze.

> For all can change in twenty four long hours
> from ice and snow to fragrant hints of flowers.

This sonnet won 1st prize in the Writing Magazine 'numbers' challenge in 2017

Unbalanced Equation

They were running on concrete
not close to the wind
or the soot of poor quality
pallid of skin
with eyes like crushed glass
not seeing the shadows
of lights while they flashed
mashing thoughts through their brain sieves
could stop them

In tracks left by
leopards or could they be muskrats
feeding on lemon peel
left in the garbage
they raced on through timetables
heading for nowhere
until when they got there
it whispered
'Don't touch'

And so t'was for nothing
the roar and the fury
of crossing off lists
and t-shirts of doing that
and being there
when what they were seeking
was back where they started
behind the first line

Vanishing Point

The
painter
takes his
largest brush
and in one grand titanium
sweep, the seasons change to
winter when the shadows barely meet
horizons not afraid to leave us searching for the
vanishing
point
or ask the question what is it supposed to be?
For fear of disapproval from peers whose
many tones in greys and golden ochres
turn our minds inside out with colds
and warms fighting for attention
and our feelings. Will we settle
for our own views or take
that which is offered on
the canvas platter?
The painting holds
the message
for you.

Verse 4 from 30 verses in 30 days

All the while she scrubs and vacuums
drowning worries in whining hums
folds her arms, unlocks his letters
harking back to distant drums
smoothing movements of cold linen
shaking memories of that bed
wondering what her life would be like
if she'd chosen him instead

Visiting North Uist: land of my ancestors

    Expectation
        Searching for forbears
        On a treeless island
        Few roads leading nowhere
        Scratching for just one scrap of
        Material evidence
        They were here

    Disappointment
        Anything would do
        A hint
        A clue
        A link
        Even broken
        But stones line up
        Row after row
        With no names

        Crofters' graves

    Acceptance
        The people would have known
        Which stones were their stones
        But they are all gone

    I reach down and touch the coldest

I look around at unfathomable horizons
I feel the soft salt breeze on my face
I breathe the hint of kelp in the air

This is the land of my ancestors.

Wasted on the Young

look back along the line
of life
pegged the past beneath
find memories once lost in
scattered days
of storms or cobalt skies

shirts and skirts and pedal-pushers
of wasted youth
bring back the days when
pulses pattered
like rain
on folded canvas fields

leave stones and other artifacts
alone, unwashed
where once we lay
with cider bottles
and Buddy Holly
raining in your heart

Watching Over You

My arms are the branches
reaching to touch your face
my body, gnarled I know
will tumble soon from grace
as barnacles and tumours
have filled that special space
where once I held your seed
will no more tempt embrace

In this garden of remembrance
where roses twine the wall
I stand as I have ever done
upright strong and tall
although my flesh is wasted now
I'm stronger than you all
watching from my lofty perch
'til you too hear the call

Were You Once an Art Teacher? Really?

If they can hold a pencil they can draw, she said
they must have certificates, she said.
The job is yours, said the pink-cheeked,
French headmistress
elegantly
from her bed
on the balcony
looking down
through scrolled wrought-iron railings
on her tiny school in Curepipe.
So teach them art,
she said.

*

Your students were offspring of sugar barons
they knew for certain what their futures held
college or no college they would still have jobs:

family sugar fields always needed bosses.

You didn't teach them to draw
nor paint — not even hold a pencil at first.

Together you followed the certificate curriculum
like spiders spinning ragged free webs
like mongooses crawling haphazard through sugar fields

you wove your way to art using the familiar
discovering how to look and see
to feel black porous lava
sculptures from
The Kanaka crater
finding nature's art.

Finally you painted
with them. En plein air
prostrate
eyes deep in the earth
looking
seeking
seeing
beneath

the Daliesque
roots of the sugar cane.

What would one need in a poem?

One would like to see the shape of sounds
around the capes and cloaks of words
bespoke even — made up syllables
to offer readers or the listener
a vision instead of readymades
on plates of verses

One would like to feel the furs and grits
of smooths with roughs of journeys
where the poem takes
readers or the listener
to a touch of sense
on open palms

One would like to hear beneath the well-known
rhymes and rhythms de-da-de-dum-de-da-de-dum
with drums and beats and breaths between
the listener's ears
pulsate at fears
the poem will end

But no
the poem never can in truth
end like that with beats and strokes
but linger in the mind that sees
and feels and hears over and
over for a lifetime.

Who cares but you?

You see the error of the way you start to write
first in your head while driving maybe
or walking. Or washing dishes.
But no real subject — just thoughts:
precious, over-enthusiastic passion
words, come on words, where are you
come and grab me
before elusiveness causes me to google.
One more time

Aging poets must do this all the time
you think
knowing there's always a better word
that comes at the wrong time like
3 am
or in the bath:
you take your first-finger nail and thumb
write it on the soap
slipping away beneath warm water's scum
and good bubbles of recollect.

'Sleep on it' you tell yourself:
'come back to it tomorrow.'
But essences of messages so personal
will drift away, you know
tomorrow's passion will take you elsewhere

You get a grip
of the poem, the message, the essence
wrong words or what
or not. You grab it.
Write it while the soup boils over.
Who cares but you?

Really.

Your forest

Sadness feels above for reaching arms
in woolly comfort.
These trees calm themselves with gentle rain
soothing bathing coolness.

Hopeful gazes through the greying vapour
drifting up to stout strong oaks.
Revealing aging wisdom in the mist
providing constant answers.

Laughter swirls in ashes through young birches
in their silver skins.
Budding hazel not yet bearing bronzing fruit
curls around the converse heaven.

The forest holds all answers if you seek
accept without a doubt.
Breathe in the fragrance that is proffered
taste tender sweet solutions as they touch upon your tongue.

The April 2020 Collection

The following 25 poems were written during the changing time that was COVID-19. In the third week of April a horrifying shooting of innocent people took place in Nova Scotia. At that point my writing shifted.

He stands before his own front door, his mother's son for sure
but speaks in his father's voice: all assurance, calm
behind the door his wife is sick.

He speaks to us, yes, all of us
then says, 'It's a bit brisk,'
darts indoors
to get a coat
before he tells us,
'Go home.
Stay home.
It is your duty.
It is your way to serve your country.'

Online/pickup grocery shopping

Peppers 1 green 1 red 1 yellow
2 lbs cake and pastry flour
no clementines no substitutes
4 pkts raspberry jello
1 pt fresh raspberries

The list seems strange
no particular logic
or is it

Imagine the aisles
Kate over there
Gail on checkout
oops we need pears

Chocolate digestives
brown rice flour
milk, cream, Devon custard
pound cake
broccoli

Parked in assigned spot
Phoned — 'we are here'
boy in long yellow raincoat like a gaucho
brings them in the pouring rain

opens the hatch back 'no don't get out'
smiles
drops the pound cake
smiles

Powerless night

There was a storm last night
the roar of wind and bowing trees
and horizontal rain
seemed worse when
power failed at ten
no normal hum of household
to mask the screaming storm

In the light of day we find
missing shingles from the roof
and leak-runs down the wall
the power's back
the rain has eased
the house's hum of life
restored

Balancing

High wire
Balancing
Safety versus stability

High risk
Balancing
Masked or unmasked

High hopes
Balancing
Statistics and reality

High skies
Balancing
Ground level action

High fives
Balancing
Touchless love

Safety
Mask
Statistics
Ground
Touchless

Corona

The holes will close if soon I do not wear
my earrings with their gold and silver hooks
There seems no need to put on fancy gear
as no-one's there to even give a fuck

The world is stopped so will it then reverse?
And turn us back to how things used to be?
Before this curse. Before the universe
created greed for more and more. Do we

stop, hear the silence, listen for new sounds
of people clapping cheering for those who
help, who heal, who feed, with love abounds
And you will know that they will see us through

>   I will sport the bling and dazzle you with diamonds
>   sing so your music will drown the sirens

Birthday party

November's not the best time for a birthday. Each year it's either fog or rain or snow, you know, but remember, remember and all that snazzy jazz pizazz. You've sent home-invented invitations, intimations of the big seven-oh with promises of lobster.

Weather did what the weather does. But worse. A curse? Lobster boats didn't go, heavens opened, deluges dragged the guests in like refugees bedraggled and besoaked. Mouths moistened for lobster. Disappointment turned to joy as smoked salmon to the rescue, urgent, couriered from New Brunswick.

The ukulele band struck up a tune — five foot two, eyes of blue, smiling eyes all round when announced by young friends: a baby in the spring, the perfect gift.

On the highway that night, an accident, one death. It feels like a trade somehow.

The bluesman plays, *Ain't no sunshine when you've gone.* The cake is cut, the candles blown.

Gifts

Kindness abounds in this place right here
it embraces the heart and reduces the fear
when gifts of the best kind arrive from the blue
proving true friendship will always win through

So thank you to Frances and to Merrill as well
and to your big bull that you needed to kill
Tilly, young Aksel and our big girl Lucy
wag tails and give kisses with hopes that we'll soon be

back to our normal but it will be different
friendships like yours — so very significant
so here's to you both, your big bull and all
we'll have a great party sometime in the fall.

Encyclopaedia

concealed ideal policy
laconic laced calico
caned conical copied

yelped icecap decoy
iced panel oceanic
iconic canopied pinacle

caped pony lion
pylon cyclone lined
cycled dice cyanide

licence lean peal
cyclopean delicacy piled
panic deep pelican

candy piece copy
cynical cancel clip
icy pine policed

Encyclopaedia

Last night

Last night I popped a pill
To see if sleep would take me
From this place of all or nothing
At least to dream

Last night I placed a call
To see if he was at the end
To talk of much but something's better
Than nothing

Last night I switched on the box
To watch the news or an old Frost
But nothing's changed just numbers
With no meaning

Today I saw the sun come up
The storm last night has blown away
Some trees are down but nothing else
Has changed

Relationships

Pairs eat posh plants
historians are pianists
their poets notes shine
snipes tailspin heroin

Lassies strain senior petals
praises his leaps tears
pilots inherit teashops
silent ratholes spoilers

Sparse lashes sharp earshot
Spanish sister polishes
orphans snore has satin
sloths its hat is thorns

Hairiness polarises hearts
epilation spirals loins
penis opts her harp
pliers paint hints heliports

Horsetails inspire parson
pristine hospitals pleats
topsails hear sin noises
alerts hessian pantries ripen.

Relationships

Jumbled

Photos of Mum — she looks like an angel
Songs from the past — cakes on the table
Films of nostalgia — escape from the now
Into another world — dreams will allow

Banishing speculations of the could-bes and maybes
remembering your strength — you were a war baby
When food was so rationed — just 2 eggs per week
Grey smog enveloped you — the outlook was bleak

But out came the sun with songs to be sung
Loughborough's carillon had bells to be rung
We'll get there again with spirit and fortitude
Patience and sense to a fresh world renewed.

This is the time

With thanks and apologies to W H Davies

This is a life now full of care,
we have the time to stand and stare.
Time to stop and watch the clouds
and stand like statues without crowds.
We now can see the wood for trees,
observing very clever bees
soar and circle then return
showing us we've much to learn
about this world as well we might
take time to find sweet nature's right
to fresh clean air, to give a chance
for seas to cleanse, how they will dance.
So let's give this life all of our care
and take the time to stand and stare.

Breviloquent

Is today's word. It popped up right after reading
Margaret Atwood's famous words
Short form: kill the ocean, and there goes your oxygen supply.

She's talking of the planet and how the world is killing it
And when this pandemic is over
Will we have listened?

Short form. Breviloquent.

The gift of time for Wendell

In the grand scheme of things when it snows in April
do you curse or bless the universe for
the poor man's fertiliser the oldies knew?

The oldies — who knew the way through.

You gaze skyward trance-like
as blossoms bud on maple trees
watch lichen drift in spring breezes.

Is that the time? Where did it go?

In the grand scheme of things
time is what you have.
In plenty.

Time gives you the gift of patience.
Patience gives you the gift of time.

Patience and time:
— the new non-hustle
— the new non-rush hour
— the new brave world
— the new way through

Like the oldies. Who knew.

Baking bread

Can a poet write while baking bread
kneading and working dough
while the words take shape
like Emily Dickinson who won prizes
for her cornmeal rye loaf

You see the world through your hands
not hers as you watch the birds
through the kitchen window
leaving your bread to rise

The spot is warm enough — but the poem?
Still words trickle as you look for
What you have:
Molasses and butter
Raisins and salt.

Bread dough shape prize loaf
Hands birds window rise

In the grand scheme of things (2)

It is no way devastating when the online pickup order
Is missing yellow peppers and yeast

It would have been
in another time
it would have been
when such things were important

But yesterday in a tiny village
2 hours away people were gunned
Down.
Killed.
by a madman.

Those folks probably had yellow peppers and yeast in their kitchen yesterday
So probably did the fifty-something professional turned murderer

So today — in the grand scheme of things
You ask yourself what really matters?

When

When did your hands
become old woman's hands?
When did those eyes
That look at you from your morning mirror
become your mother's eyes?

She questions you now
The little upturned 'W' furrow
The cocking of her white-haired head
She who gave you this life

Did we do well with the life?
You ask of her
Did we do our best?

We did what we thought was right and good at the time
Is her reply
We found the best way forward
Made decisions (right or wrong)
Or somewhere in between

You look again at your arthritic fingers
Wrinkled hands with raised veins that still pump
Life

You look her in the eyes now
Looking into your own
And nod.

In that moment — the unfinished poem

In that moment when
You meander the trail
Stop to listen to the evening peepers
Gasp at the sunset
Is the moment when all life is taken from you

In that moment when
You stand at your kitchen stove
Frying eggs for supper, maybe a little crispy Canadian bacon
You breathe in the aroma of comfort
Is the moment when all life is taken from you

In that moment when
You lift your fiddle in your teen basement
And thump out a Nova Scotia jig
Tapping your feet with love
Is the moment when all life is taken from you

In that moment when
You sit on your stoop and scratch your loyal dog's floppy ears
And plan your next virtual class with your students
Sip a glass of rose wine, breathe deeply
Is the moment when all life is taken from you

Written following the mass shooting in a small rural community in Nova Scotia April 19/20 2020

An April Week in a Nova Scotia Garden

There's a short window of time
between the frost leaving the ground
And the blackflies arriving in their
evil swarms

Soft April warmth
buds showing brief tips
like sharp green-tinged noses saying,
"Hi."
It's time to restore the garden
from the ravages of winter
To coddle it into the new season
To see what has survived
And what has not.

The wisteria was planted twenty five years ago
What a monster it has become
The dominant
The strangler
The throttler
The tangler
Tentacles over thirty feet long
wrists thicker than my thigh

We cut and hack untwist and
mourn the loss of this and that dear shrub:
The bronze azalea

The sweet aromatic Klondyke rhododendron
The Siberian Maple
The Philadelphus
The Corkscrew Hazel, we've yet to see what else

Each day a new discovery
Each day applauding the survivors:
Magnolia: Stellata, Susan, Seiboldii

Sequoia, Bamboo, Weeping Nootka
Tangutika, we've yet to see what else

But those that have met their demise will
Live on in our memories

St. George's Day

Time to slay the dragons on this
St. George's Day
We'll beat the sadness filling us
We do not have to pay

For evil done by others
Driv'n by craziness
It's time to rise beyond above
And find the finer goodness

In flowers op'ning up their buds
As birds still build their nests
The clouds scud by the world still turns
To put our minds at rest

Not all has stopped just ask St. George
The dragons' fires will out
We'll carry on the best we can
And smile without a doubt.

The response to the bridge challenge

Look up — shout out — see the sunrise
Fragmenting through the trees of spring
Stretching gold apricot vermillion reaching
Giving new life
Giving deep thoughts
Giving fresh hope

Letters of Distraction

Electricity

Try celery tie city
Elicit cleric eye erect
Tyre relit icily

Reel elite celerity
Recite recycle trite
Elect electric tricycle

Yet trice tile icicle
Tree let lyre cry
Eery eel rice circle

Electricity

Individual

Livid Dad undid anvil
Unlaid dial inlaid nail
Invalid lad and van

Vain diva divan laid
Land add dual iliad
Arid and valid aid lain

Did lid din via Uni.

Individual

The lesson

There is no scar on the blueness above
No thrum of a motor
No hum of a bus
Instead there is peace and a clearness we'd lost

Not just the birds sing
The earth is alive
The flora
The fauna
All nod like the wise
Who foretold this
in history
or only last year

To turn off and look out
Look up and look in
A lesson in mending
of stopping the greeding
And letting the heed
Take us from here.

The Last of the Month

The last of the month
The first of the day
The bread is now riz
But what can I say
The yeast that was rare
Is now here in plenty
And too much went in
To this dough in a frenzy

The month that is over
Will never return
As frugal's now normal
no money to burn
We use what we have
If we haven't we can't
We can dig for the future
And think of the past

This plight of the world will go down in books
There'll be clever recipes and simple crafts
From rookie designers and cooks
The garden will blossom like never before
And the bees will come back
We know this for sure
The bats in the belfries
Will ring loud the bells
To tell us it's over
But never the same

Remember these clear skies
Clean waters beneath
Repairing this world
Came out of need
Let's not forget
How easy things fell
How easy neglect
Sent us almost to hell

Now COVID is drifted
Away with the newsreaders
We'll tell our own stories
Of how we came through.

Vapour trail

One chalk line across unblemished skies
is this a tip-toeing back with one tentative
tender mark?

There once were many — too many
strident — non-hesitant — confident
criss-crossing — scratching — cross-hatching
scarring — blemishing blue with white
bringing — taking — striking

fading

constant streams of vapour through an invisible constellation

Since March there have been none

now here is one — the first
streaking from east to west
a single filament strand of hair
from the underbelly of a soft white dog

leaving behind a spreading trail of vapour

Acknowledgements

I'm thankful for my love of poetry. For my collection of poetry books that I dip into for more reasons than I can list here. Gosh, I'm so thankful I learned to read when I was four.

I write, for the most part, without conscious thought and thank Canadian author, playwright and poet, Susan Musgrave whose workshop all those years ago left its mark. It was she who taught me to seek out the essence of the message. Like a good balsamic glaze reduction.

My thanks also go to the poet Hugo Williams who drew my attention to line endings, and to Alex Pierce for the six-week poetry workshop at The Riverbank.

To the literary journals and magazines around the world that gave my work homes over the years, the best validation a poet could ask. Thank you.

A giant thank you goes to my writer family: the members (past and present) of the international online writing group for expats, Writers Abroad, especially the talented poets, Chris, Bruce, Pattie, John and Jax.

Jack — and by association, Leonard Cohen, who caused my literary corner to turn in 2009 with the inclusion of my contribution, *Sister of No Mercy* (page 105) in *Leonard Cohen You're Our Man*. RIP both. Eternal gratitude.

To Arne, for your unfailing love and support, for believing in me, for hearing my recitations, thank you for always making all things possible and for teaching me that being nosey was just fine.

Massive thanks to S.R. Stewart and all at Unsolicited Press for taking me on, making my collection come alive, and for making the process an absolute joy. And for letting me keep my English spelling.

And finally, thank you to this peaceful corner of the world, where thinking, observing, dreaming and writing poetry can happen.

About the Author

S.B. Borgersen is a British/Canadian author, of middle England and Hebridean ancestry, whose favoured genres are flash and micro fiction, and poetry.

Sue was educated at diverse institutions including boarding at a French convent in Nicosia, Cyprus before transferring in 1958 to a boarding school for military brats where she published her first story, *My Life Story: told by Laika, the Sputnik Dog* in *The Crusader*, the first magazine of King Richard School, Dhekelia, Cyprus.

Sometime after that was the freedom of The North Warwickshire School of Art.

She had a diverse career path, an analyst in a shoe factory, the same thing for a children's book publisher, teaching art, and filing for the civil service, but mostly she climbed a precarious ladder in the IT industry culminating in strategy and project management, which, by necessity in those days, included writing writing writing mountains of non-fiction — always allowing herself to be slightly creative with proposals, reports, technical and training documentation.

Sue turned her back on industry and commerce in the early nineties, escaping the stressful rat-race and finding the simple life and peaceful place she'd always sought to allow for creativity. That place was Nova Scotia where she returned to her skills from art school and made an uncomplicated living as a visual artist and potter. That is, until she got the creative writing bug.

Since 2000 her writing has won prizes, been mentioned in Hansard and published internationally in literary journals and anthologies (print and online). Her latest full-length books, *Fishermen's Fingers* and *While the Kettle Boils* were released in 2020 by Unsolicited Press. The list of publications is extensive and can be found at www.sueborgersen.com

She is a loyal member of The Writers' Federation of Nova Scotia and an enthusiastic member of the international online writers' group for expats, Writers Abroad. She is also a newish member of The Society of Authors.

Sue lives in a crumbling old house on the shores of Nova Scotia with her patient husband and a clutch of lovable rowdy dogs. She has two middle-aged children.

S.B. Borgersen writes every day.

About the Press

Unsolicited Press was founded in 2012 and is based in Portland, Oregon. The small press publishes fiction, poetry, and creative nonfiction written by award-winning and emerging authors. Some of its authors include John W. Bateman, Anne Leigh Parrish, Adrian Ernesto Cepeda, and Raki Kopernik.

Learn more at www.unsolicitedpress.com